LESS THAN HALF,
MORE THAN WHOLE

BY *Kathleen and Michael Lacapa*

ILLUSTRATED BY *Michael Lacapa*

rising moon

Books for Young Readers from Northland Publishing

The illustrations in this book were done in guache and pen and ink
on Fabriano Classico 300 lb. hot press watercolor paper.
The display type was set in M Castellar.
The text type was set in Bembo.
Composition by Northland Publishing, Flagstaff, Arizona.
Printed and bound by South Sea International Press, Ltd., Hong Kong.
Production supervised by Lisa Brownfield.
Designed by Rudy J. Ramos.
Edited by Kathryn Wilder.

FIRST EDITION, 1994
Second Printing, 1996
ISBN 0-87358-592-5

First Softcover Printing, 1998
ISBN 0-87358-734-0

Library of Congress Catalog Card Number 94-13132
Cataloging-in-Publication Data
Lacapa, Kathleen. 1959-
Less than half, more than whole / by Kathleen and Michael Lacapa. — 1st ed.
p. cm.
1. Indian of North America—Juvenile fiction.
[1. A child who is only part Native American is troubled
by his mixed racial heritage.
2. Indians of North America—Fiction. 3. Individuality—Fiction.]
I. Lacapa, Michael, ill. II. Title.
PZ7.L117Le 1994
[E]—dc20
94-13132

0719/2.5M/7-98

To Daniel, Rochelle, and Anthony,

the greatest gifts we have received, or will ever receive;

and to all children: May you know that you are "more than whole."

—K. L. & M. L.

Listen!

The wind blowing across the lake carried
the sounds of reeds bending . . . water lapping . . .
stones skipping . . . boys laughing.

"Hey, guys! I found a great stone," said Tony,
letting the flat rock spin out of his fingers. It skipped
and bounced across the lake.

"Let me try," said Scott. The three friends
laughed and yelled as each stone went flying.

Suddenly, the boys eyed the perfect stone lying in the shallow water. Three hands reached toward it at once. "Wait!" Tony yelled. He stared into the lake. "Look, guys, I can see our faces." Each boy peered at the face reflecting back at him off the water.

As the lake grew still, the boys saw the color of their hair, eyes, and skin. Scott's hair was yellow, and his eyes were the color of the sky. Will's skin was brown, and his hair black as night. Tony saw that he wasn't as dark as Will or as light as Scott.

Will and Scott noticed this, too. "You're not like me," Will said. "I'm all Indian. I think you're only half, or less than half."

A mother's voice broke through the sounds of wind in the reeds and lapping water: "Time to come home!" The boys left, each going in his own direction.

Less than half, less than half—the words ran through Tony's mind. "What does that mean?" he said aloud. But he heard nothing; even the wind was quiet now. He felt the ground rising under his feet, and found that he was wandering toward his Grandma Doris's house.

Grandma Doris sat working in her garden. Bees and butter-flies bobbed around her head. "Well, hello there, Tony," she said as he knelt down next to her in the cool brown dirt. Her garden smelled like sun and rain and growing things.

In a sad voice Tony said, "Hi, Grandma."

Grandma Doris stopped working and asked, "What's wrong?"

"Grandma, I don't look like Scott or Will, and Will says I'm less than half. What does that mean, less than half?"

Grandma Doris picked a purple flower and gave it to him. "Hold this very still," she said. Without a sound, a butterfly landed lightly on the flower in Tony's hand. Grandma Doris whispered, "This butterfly is special, just like you. See the pattern on its wings, and all the colors? The colors make it different, and beautiful."

The breeze lifted the butterfly high into the sky. Tony watched it until he could no longer see it.

"You'd better run on home," Grandma Doris said. "Your father will be looking for you soon."

Tony left the garden and walked toward his house, thinking about the butterfly and what his grandmother had said. But he didn't have his answer. What was less than half?

Dusty feet . . . panting breath . . . a loud slam of the door.

Tony was home, and ready to ask his question again.

His brother and sister sat in the living room. Rochelle looked up from tying her tennis shoes and called out, "Tony's home!"

Daniel turned and asked, "Where've you been?"

"I was down at the water skipping stones," Tony said. "What does it mean when someone says you're half, or less than half?" He watched as his brother and sister looked at each other. They knew what he meant because they had asked this question when they were young.

"It means you are not all one race," his sister said. "We are part Indian, and part Anglo." Then she added under her breath, "Sometimes you wonder where you belong."

"Ah, don't worry about it," said Daniel. "You can't change who you are. Come on, Rochelle, let's go shoot some hoops."

Tony was left feeling more confused than ever. "Sometimes a brother and sister are no help!" he said to himself.

His mother called from the hallway: "Get washed up, Tony. We're going to Saiya and TáTdá's house for supper." Saiya and TáTdá were Tony's grandmother and grandfather who lived on the reservation. He loved going to their house. Saiya, TáTdá, and all his cousins would be there. His uncle with the horses would be there, too.

As soon as the car came to a stop, Tony jumped out and headed down the canyon toward the horse corral where his uncle was feeding the horses. Swishing tails . . . stomping hooves . . . rising dust. The noises the horses made sounded strange as they echoed off the canyon walls.

"Hey, Tony, good to see you!" said his uncle. "Come, help me feed the horses." Tony and his uncle worked side by side throwing hay into the corral.

"Uncle," said Tony, "which horse do you like best?"

Tony's uncle stopped and leaned against the corral. He was quiet for a long time. Finally, he pointed to a horse in the corner. "I like that one over there," he said. "It is strong and proud, and has a lot of good markings. Without its different colors, it would not seem so special." He turned to Tony with a smile in his eyes. "It reminds me of you!"

Tony looked at the horse and thought about his uncle's words. Saiya's voice came floating down the canyon: "Time to eat!"

Saiya always had good food. Chili bread, hominy stew, and fry bread covered the table. Chewing . . . chatting . . . laughter . . . warm smiles filled the air.

Tony sat and ate his food quietly, watching the faces around the table. When he had eaten the last of his fry bread, he was stuffed. "My stomach is too full," he said. "Can I go lay down?"

TáTdá said, "Go ahead and lay on my bed. I'll check on you soon."

The bedroom was filled with many things. Bows and baskets . . . pottery and corn . . . pictures hanging from every wall. An old mirror rested on TáTdá's dresser. Tony stared into it. "Less than half—why am I less than half?" he said to his reflection.

A voice from behind him said, "I like what I see, don't you?"

"TáTdá, I don't look like everyone else. My hair is not black. My eyes are not the color of the sky. Will said that I am less than half."

"This is true. You are not like anyone else." TáTdá sat down on the bed next to Tony and looked at him in the mirror. "Your mother's skin is light, and your father's skin is dark." He pointed to the photographs around the mirror. Round faces, long faces, some old, some young . . . short people, fat people, people who could touch the sky . . . dark skin, light skin, and some just in between. Tony's picture was there, too.

TáTdá said, "These are the faces of our family. None are alike, but each is special. And they are all a part of you." Tony listened carefully.

TáTdá pointed to a bundle of corn hanging on the wall. "Do you see this corn? It is a gift from the Creator. He gave it to our people so we could survive in this land."

"He did not give this gift only in one color but in many colors. I keep this bundle here so I will remember the gift the Creator has given me—my family of many colors."

TáTdá untied one ear of corn from the bundle. Its colors were red, purple, and blue with white speckles.

"This corn is like you," Tony's grandfather said. "It is one of great beauty because of its many colors. And just as the corn with its many colors is a gift to the people, so you are a gift from the Creator.

"Some will see only the blue in this ear of corn, and others will see only the red, but I do not see anything less than a whole ear of corn and all that it means to our people. You are not half a person because of your color, my son; you are a whole, beautiful person."

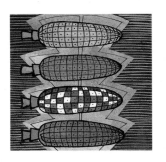

Tony looked into his grandfather's eyes in the mirror framed by all the different sizes, shapes, and colors of his family. Finally, he understood: He was not less than half; he—like the corn— was more than whole.

THE END

Glossary of Concepts, Terms, and Designs

The characters in *Less Than Half, More Than Whole* come from many different ethnic backgrounds. The designs in the illustrations represent these various cultures.

CONCEPTS:

Saiya's house: In many Native American societies, the women own the property and home. The home is referred to as "Grandmother's house."

The number four: Tony goes to four different locations to find the answer to his question. Four is an important number in many Native cultures. It symbolizes the four seasons, the four directions, and perfection. When anything of spiritual significance is undertaken, it is performed in increments of four.

Corn: According to Hopi legend, corn was the first gift given to them from the Creator. It symbolizes life, and, because of its many colors, represents all races.

Grandfather/Elder: Many Native peoples view their elders as keepers of wisdom, culture, and history. Elders are given great respect.

TERMS:

Saiya: Tewa word for Grandmother, pronounced "Sahee-YAH."

TáTdá: Tewa word for Grandfather, pronounced something like "Dah-Dah," with a consonant sound between a "T" and a "D" (a sound not used in English).

DESIGNS:

Prehistoric Pueblo design found in rock art, representing water.

Hopi bear symbol with Apache medicine bag in the background. This symbolizes Daniel's Tewa name, "White Bear" (which means Strong Medicine).

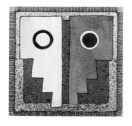

Split feather pattern found in Hopi and Tewa pottery designs.

Tewa spider design, Apache cross symbol, and Mohawk water lily design. This symbolizes Rochelle's Tewa name, "Grandma Spider" (which means Helper).

Blue bird on Apache star symbolizes Tony's Tewa name, "Blue Bird Boy." Corners from Apache medicine bag, blue bird from Anasazi petroglyphs.

Apache basket design representing horses.

Hopi butterfly design with Mohawk water lily in the background.

Athapaskan horse pictograph on Apache star pattern.

Sikyatki pottery butterfly design.

Hopi Tewa spider design with feather pattern and Apache basket patterns.

 Apache basket patterns and medicine bag patterns, with bear paw symbol representing the Bear Clan, Saiya's clan.

 Rain bird design with plume found on Hopi Tewa pottery. Plume represents spirit life.

 Blue bird pattern found on Anasazi rock art. Background designs are from Mohawk tattoos.

 Hopi corn design found in basket designs.

 Hopi bird patterns found on rock art. Split feather design found on Hopi Tewa pottery.

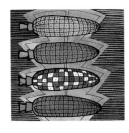 Hopi corn design as seen on coiled basketry.

 The growing process—soil and rain connected by a cornstalk—as represented by cloud patterns and growing corn patterns. These, and blue bird, are Hopi designs found on rock art.

KATHLEEN LACAPA joined her husband, MICHAEL, in writing *Less Than Half, More Than Whole* for their three children, Rochelle, Anthony, and Daniel, and for all children who come from multicultural backgrounds and struggle with the question, "Where do I belong?" Kathleen is of Irish, English, and Mohawk descent, and Michael is Apache, Hopi, and Tewa. They both work with school-age children in and around the White Mountain Apache Reservation, and live with their children in Taylor, Arizona. Michael launched his career as an illustrator with *The Mouse Couple* (1988), and went on to write and illustrate the award-winning *The Flute Player* (1990) and *Antelope Woman* (1992). *Less Than Half, More Than Whole* is Kathleen's first children's book.